Love

Love

DONNA
ASHWORTH

BLACK & WHITE PUBLISHING

First published in the UK in 2022 by
Black & White Publishing Ltd
Nautical House, 104 Commercial Street, Edinburgh, EH6 6NF

A division of Bonnier Books UK
4th Floor, Victoria House, Bloomsbury Square, London, WC1B 4DA
Owned by Bonnier Books
Sveavägen 56, Stockholm, Sweden

Interior illustrations copyright © Zephyr Cliparts via Creative Market.

A CIP catalogue record for this book is available from the British Library.

ISBN: 978 1 78530 440 8

3 5 7 9 10 8 6 4

Typeset by Iolaire Typesetting, Newtonmore
Printed and bound in Great Britain by Clays Ltd, Elcograf S.p.A.

www.blackandwhitepublishing.com

I dedicate this book to my friends. Those I know inside out, and those who support me from afar. Of all the types of love, mystically weaving their way around this planet, your cheerleading kind is the fire in my engine on days when coal is scarce. And I value you wildly.

AUTHOR'S NOTE

This is not simply a book of love poetry, for the romantics among us. This is a book for anyone who has a beating heart. For anyone who has ever known the joy and pain of family, friendship, love and loss. In short, this book is for *everyone*. Because what are we here to do, if not love?

CONTENTS

CONTENTS

Author's note   vii

Love is the answer   3
Listen for the love   5
On your wedding day   6
Your circle   9
Friendships   11
A mother's love   13
Love doesn't hurt   14
Love grows   17
Be in love   18
If your mother did not love you   20
Root or run   22
Don't love by half   25
Look   27
Breaking the chain   29
The teenage cloud   31
Revenge body   33
Home   34
Moths   37
To feel loved   39
Here's to the friends   41
Love too much   43
A friend like you   45
The love of a dog   47

Revenge   49
That soul connection   52
Nice   55
Control   57
The solo valentine   59
Ordinary love   60
Many moons   63
Heart like glass   65
Be kind to yourself too   67
Dusty lens   69
Loving   71
Oceans and streams   73
It will be you   75
For a lifetime   77
To love yourself   79
Let them rest   81
Only you   83
Strangers   85
To love your daughter   87
Little man   89
Dear sister   91
Dandelion seeds   95
Love will not spoil   97
Go little   99
To a flower   101
Attention   103
Let joy stay high   105
The lost friends   107
Alone is not unloved   109
Wherever I go   111
The choosing   113
Tomorrow   114
Frosting   117
How you grow   119
Rot   121

Unspoken truths   123
Into the ground   125
Close to the sun   127
Love is all around   129
Torch in my pocket   131
Someone   135
Love is the goal   136
Didn't waste a day   138
She screamed   141

Acknowlegements   143

there is no such thing

as too much love

but your own

is all you truly need

LOVE IS THE ANSWER

When I say that love is the answer
I mean it
you have to love
with every inch of your soul.

Love your people
love them as though your love is the answer
because it *is*.

Love *things*
not material things
things that come for free
and when you find the things
that you particularly love
love the heck out of them.

Get passionate
every day
about things which spark your spirit.

LOVE your life
love your LIFE.

You're not here to walk on broken glass
you're here to find your joy
so find it
in every moment you can.

When I say that love is the answer
I mean it.

LISTEN FOR THE LOVE

We don't always say *I love you*
sometimes we say
You're not eating very well
or *Should you be going out in this weather?*

We don't always say
You're amazing.
Sometimes we say
I wish you would believe in yourself more.

We don't always say *I love you.*
Sometimes, we open our mouths
and our hearts
(which are actually full of love)
pour out critically
nagging, berating, moaning, smothering.

We can work on that.

Sometimes, love doesn't always sound like
I love you.
Sometimes it sounds like
Eat more vegetables
Be home by 9
Don't work so hard.

Listen for the love in everything you hear today
it doesn't always sound like it should.
But it's there.
It's there.

ON YOUR WEDDING DAY

It was love that made you
love that raised you
and with love
we are here today
to watch you carry it on.

You see
we are not about to *give you away*
for love is not something
one *can* give away
it is always there
always growing
always producing more love
in its wake.

We are here today
to see you
create *more* love
and watch that miracle unfold
because that's what we raised you to do
love.

Well done to you
for taking the love we all grew together
and finding another
to share that with
to grow even more love with.

We are proud
beyond proud
we are complete.

Because that is how
you came into this world
loved
so very loved
and you will never live a day
unloved.

You will never live a day
not being loved
little one.

What could be better than that?

YOUR CIRCLE

Your circle
should have no edges
your circle
should continuously flow
as circles do
passing energy
to one another
taking
when needed
and giving
when abundant.

Your circle
should want you to win
your circle
should want to see you shine
and when you don't shine
your circle
should direct their flow of light
a little more your way.

Your circle
should have no edges my friend
because circles
must be round.

Smooth out any edges
in your circle
and watch that flow
do wonderful things for you all.

FRIENDSHIPS

I don't think friendships
are given enough credit.

We sign no contract
we say no vows
and yet we are there for each other

for better or for worse
in sickness and in health.

We laugh together
in life-giving amounts
we cry together
without shame.

We pull each other up
out of the mud
again
and again
and again.

I don't think friendships
are given enough credit.

Unwritten love stories
each and every one.

A MOTHER'S LOVE

A mother's love
lives in the gut
deep
deep within the gut.

Deep down
where the soul shakes hands with instinct
where the present-day combines
with intuition honed by ancestors.

That's where a mother's love lives.

A mother's love is fierce
primal
cellular
built-in
everlasting
mountain-moving
barrier-breaking
standard-shaking.

If you dare to challenge
this age-old energy
prepare to witness
humanity
at its strongest.

There is nothing more
nothing *deeper*
than a mother's love.

LOVE DOESN'T HURT

Love really shouldn't hurt
loss hurts
abuse hurts
poor behaviour hurts
unrequited love hurts.

But love
in its purest
and simplest form
should feel like a safety net
like a bridge over troubled water
like *coming home*.

Behaviour hurts
love doesn't
love sees straight to the soul
you can't turn it on or off
even death can't break it.

If your **love**
is causing you pain
something is wrong
very wrong.

You deserve to be loved
unconditionally
in this life
if you have to earn it
chase it
or you constantly fear losing it
this is not your love story.

If you are scared to
break the bonds
of this 'love'
that's bringing you hurt
don't be
the love you have for yourself
will take its place
for what could be a greater act of self-love
than to set yourself free.

Free to find even more love.

Real love.

LOVE GROWS

You don't fall in and out of love
love *endures*
you fall in and out of like
you fall in and out of infatuation
you fall in and out of lust
you fall in and out of friendship.

You don't fall in and out of love
ask anyone
who has lost someone
too soon
they will tell you
love *endures*.

Even when the final memory
of that person
has dissipated
the love for their very soul is
passed down
genetically imprinted
into cells
unending.

You don't fall in and out of love
that's romance
friendship.

Love
real love
only grows
it never goes

BE IN LOVE

Be in love
with your life
every minute
it's your trail
blaze it and blaze it brightly.

Be in love
with yourself
think of how you'd like to be loved
and make it happen
show the way for others.

Be in love
with your partner
really love them
as if there were no tomorrow
and all you have is
right here right now.

Be in love
with your home
never mind the mess
the things you don't like
pour some sparkle
on what you have.

Be in love
with your family
none are perfect
but they are your blood
and your history
you need each other in this life.

Be in love
with your job
look at all the positives
and be thankful you have it
if you can't
then change it
life's too short.

Be in love
with being in love
create that life
full of friendship
stolen kisses
unnecessary hugs
food for the soul.

IF YOUR MOTHER DID NOT LOVE YOU

If your mother did not love you
the way she *could* have
your heart is never
quite full.

If your mother was not always
who she may have been
your soul is somehow
incomplete.

If your inner little girl
was not taught how to feel
your journey is
not easy my friend

but you owe it to that little girl
to learn
you owe it to her
to *create* love
you owe it to her
to build a world so full of love
that it will eventually outshadow
the demons of your past.

And here's the thing

love *regenerates*

so make it and watch it blossom
in the hearts of those around you
and watch them pass it
on and on and on
until you have singlehandedly
made enough love
and *more*

to fill that void you carry
and to fill the voids of anyone
who is sent into your orbit.

If your mother did not love you
the way she *could* have

you have some catching up to do
but I know you will my friend
I know you will

it starts with you.

ROOT OR RUN

If you have ever been in a controlling relationship
you will know that feeling
the almost imperceptible shift
in the atmosphere around you
the halting of your breath
stopping
mid lung
waiting to exhale
the dread
the prickle of your skin
as your instincts scream
silently from within
Run
but you stay rooted
and you don't know why.

If you have ever been in a controlling relationship
you will understand exactly
and you will see the signs around you
when others root and don't run.

If you have ever known this fear my friend
and you have *run*
I am so proud of you
but I want more
though I know you've been through hell
I still want more.

I want you to watch for the ones who still root
and I want you to tell them
that it's only in the running
the cycle is broken.

There is no other way.

You cannot *behave* someone else better
you cannot get *smaller* to anger them less
they like small
they like less
they feast on it.

Watch for those who root
and don't run
one day they will
and we can help them run
faster
than they ever have
before.

DON'T LOVE BY HALF

Don't love by half
don't *play* at love
if you are going to love someone
let them feel it
let them believe
they are a precious gift
in this life
because they *are*.

Love them
the way *you* have dreamed
of being loved
because you can
so why would you not?

Loving by half is like fake laughter
it is pointless
because if you only let go
and opened your heart
you would laugh for real.

You give nothing away
by allowing your laughter to flow freely
it's the same with love.

You cannot run out of it.

So don't love by half
that's the quickest way
to waste your precious time
here on earth.

LOOK

Look how well you've done
without being shown the *way*.

Without being taught
how to exist
in a world
that wants to crush you.

Look how far you've come
without the *key*
the *manual*
the *map*.

And now you're on your way
and this time you know
you *know*
that you're not here to suffer
you know
that you're here to *thrive*.

And that you don't need
anyone else's love

if you just have
your own.

BREAKING THE CHAIN

If you are the first
of your bloodline
to break the chain
the one to say *no more*
it is little wonder
your life has felt
like a battlefront my friend
for it has been such.

But thanks to your courage
thanks to your lion heart
history will change.

You broke the dam
to send that water on
to pastures new
to pastures green.

You did that.

Look at what you have done
be proud
and sail on to your *new*
sail on to your new, sweet one.

You have much love to make.

THE TEENAGE CLOUD

Teenagers may not want to talk
but you must never stop listening
to their sounds
and their silence.

They may constantly reject
your affection
but don't you ever stop
making those moves.

Teenagers may push you far away
to see if your love is breakable
to see where the boundary
of your love lies

show them it is endless.

Hang on tight
through these wilderness years
and keep your door open.

There will be a moment
every now and again
when they need you
be there.

The teenage cloud is temporary
but much distance can be covered
stay close.

REVENGE BODY

The phrase revenge body
implies that somehow
your physical form was to blame
for whatever destroyed your world.

That by becoming smaller
or fitter
you can hurt those people
the way they hurt you.

Where do we start with this?

Your body was never the issue
and nor will it ever *be* the issue.

That relationship
was simply not right for you
and revenge is not what
you should be aiming for
sweet relief
is the emotion you should feel
once the rejection has passed.

Let your body be as it is
you beautiful creature
your *actual* life
will recognise *you*

when it is time.

HOME

To my children
whatever choices you make
in this life
wherever you go
whomever you choose
to share it with
I want you to keep
coming *home*.

I want you to know
that in this fast-paced
crazy world
in which we live
you always have a safe place
to rest your weary head
and your heart.

This door
it will never close
not to you.

I will try
with all my might
to refrain from judging you.

I get it
this is your life now
your path
and you need to walk it
your way
but I am here.

I have walked many paths too
so if you need any advice
ask me
I will always try
to see it your way.

The wonderful thing about family is
we need never face anything alone
and in that vein
anyone in your home
has a home in my home too.

Fly high
dream big
live loudly
love fiercely.

Show the world
what you are made of my love.

Show them your light
let it shine out there.

And when your light won't beam
the way it should

I will be here to help switch it back on.

Always.

MOTHS

Showing up
just as you are
without shame or fear
is like firing a flare
into the night sky
calling twin-souled tribes
into your orbit
like moths to a flame.

You won't find your people
if they don't recognise you

stay you
stay real
let them *see* your light.

Let it shine brightly
weirdly
wildly
and watch your people flock

like moths to a flame.

TO FEEL LOVED

When you were a child
all you had to do
to make someone proud
to feel loved
was nap
sleep well
play nice
and eat some greens.

I feel these should be
our self-acceptance goalposts
for adult life too.

We eat so much pressure
every day
spoon-fed to us by the world
but swallowed whole
all on our own.

Perhaps it's time
to move those goalposts
make it simple.

When you were a child
you felt loved
just by living.

You can make that so again.

HERE'S TO THE FRIENDS

Here's to the friends
who give us grace to cancel the plans we made
when we were a different version of ourselves.

Here's to the friends
who never say *I told you so*
but instead sit down
to hear the entire story
they predicted already.

Here's to the friends
who have our secrets in their pocket
and keep them safely guarded.

Here's to the friends
who show up for the happy and the sad
and see the importance in both.

Here's to the friends
we just could not be without
on this rollercoaster ride.

Here's to the friends
who bring in light
when light is scarce.

*Here's to you
and here's to them
we're blessed indeed
to have those friends.*

LOVE TOO MUCH

They told you
you love too much
but that cannot be done
in the same way
that one cannot breathe
too much

too much love does not exist

it is not a thing.

What they mean
is that they love
too little
that their love for you
is not a priority
or commitment.

Do not berate your living heart
for doing what it should

it is not you who needs to change.

You cannot love too much
but you can be more careful
who you love
so very wonderfully
next time.

A FRIEND LIKE YOU

A friend like you
is a wonderful thing
the very best gift
this life can bring
a soul who sparks with another
so deep
a partner in crime
to laugh with
to weep

A friend like you
is a mystical force
brought from
an otherworldly source
a sister not born
or chosen but gifted
a safe place to go
where vibrations are lifted

A friend like you
is a magical spell
there's no limit to
the secrets we tell
a space with no judgement
no envy, no greed
more friends like you
is what this world needs.

THE LOVE OF A DOG

If I were to be tasked
with teaching a loveless world
how to change
I would show them
the love of a dog.

Because the love of a dog
is a commitment
a decision
it is undying
unwaveringly enduring
and loyal
to the very core.

The love of a dog
is wholeheartedly forgiving
it is soul-nurturing in its purity
and utterly life-affirming.

If I were to be tasked
with teaching a loveless world
how to change
I would show them
the love of a dog.

If you do not know this love
my friend
I urge you
compel you

to seek it out.

REVENGE

Revenge is a dish best served cold
they say
but I think revenge is a dish
that should not be served at all.

Do not waste your time
grafting in that cold kitchen
making a deadly dish
to try to break their spirit
save your time and your power
to cook yourself some joy.

The best revenge
without a doubt
is no revenge at all.

You have a life to rebuild
and you are far too beautiful
to sink to their depths
when you should be climbing
to dizzy
life-alteringly
heart-burstingly
mind-blowingly
new heights.

Climb, my friend
don't sink

never sink.

Revenge is a dish
best served
straight into the bin.

how brave you are

to let others walk inside your heart

when you know the damage

that can be done in there

THAT SOUL CONNECTION

Ah but you will love *so* much
within your one lifetime
you will love many different souls
in many different ways
and your love will be the fuel
for *so* many fires.

You will love *so* much in your lifetime.

You will *be* so loved within your lifetime.

You will be loved by so many
in a variety of ways
and their love will fuel *your* fire too.

But if you have not yet learned
the greatest love of all
it will be difficult to keep those fires fuelled
to allow your own fire
to be so.

For if you do not love *you*
if you have not made
that soul connection
with yourself
then none of the above
will flow easily my friend.

Each relationship will falter and fail
or limp along bravely
but without glory
because until you open those floodgates
and allow self-love to flow

there will always be a block.

Take the time
and face the pain
and open your heart up to you
for you.

Do the work
say your apologies
make amends with the person
you abandoned long ago.

Do not wait until you are loveable
to learn to love yourself
do it now
for everyone knows true love
cares not for flaws.

Ah but you will love so much
within your one lifetime
make sure some of that love
is for you.

NICE

You don't have to love yourself
to feel peace
but you do have to try
to be nice.

You do have to give yourself
the basic respect
and dignity
you offer the rest of the world.

You (very much) do
have to *like* yourself
at least be your own friend.

Because if you can't do that
you're signing up
to a lifetime trapped
in a very toxic relationship.

And you can't walk away from this one
so give in.

Be nice.

Just, be, nice.

CONTROL

You can't control
how much the people in your life
love you
but you can control
how much *you* love you.

And that codes a pathway
for all *new* love.

You're literally teaching
everyone around you
how to love *you*
and how to love themselves too.

Let those who didn't love you go
and fill the void yourself.

You cannot turn back time
and be loved by them
but you can change the way
the future serves you.

By making the love yourself.

And once you realise
that love is limitless
there's no going back

and no desire to either.

THE SOLO VALENTINE

Perhaps Valentine's Day
could be about *counting*
counting all the love
you have in your life
and giving gratitude for it

especially if you're counting
the hard-won love
you found for yourself
along the way.

It's not all hearts and flowers
no
but it is
very much
worth celebrating.

Those friends
who take time out of their day
to check your stress levels.

The family members
who are quite wonderfully
always there
in a crisis.

You are loved.
Look around
see it
be loved
feel loved
today
and every day.

ORDINARY LOVE

Some people love
in grandness
displaying that bright love
like a fountain of fiery romance
to rain flowers forevermore
upon the apple of their eye
telling the world
this love is *extraordinary*.

And because this love
is so visibly majestic to behold
it is revered and desired
by those without it.

But some people love
in ordinary
diligently and consistently
drip-feeding their love
in nurture form
often unseen or unnoticed
rarely celebrated
always reliable.

And because this love
is so humble
it can be brushed away
as unimportant

yet without it

worlds would crumble
lives would fall apart
and souls would be forever-seeking
their flamboyant mate

whilst passing by
their very cornerstone
right under the nose.

I guess what I am trying to say is

there is no such thing as ordinary love
it is all quite amazingly
profoundly
extraordinary

whether it shouts from the rooftops
or whispers in the holding of a hand.

You just have
to see it
to make it
the wondrous entity

you seek.

MANY MOONS

Many moons
waned
and many suns
rose
before I learned
that perfect
is not found
in unspoiled skin
or the racing limb
the well-stitched bag
or the shiny jewel
the glittering career
or money in a bank
it is found
in the love

and nowhere else.

HEART LIKE GLASS

You have thought yourself
so weak
for all the shattering.

But oh there is much strength
much courage
in the way you feel
everything
so very deeply
every day.

So much power
in the way you fall apart
and come back
each and every time.

Bravery exists daily
within those

who have a
heart
like
glass.

BE KIND TO YOURSELF TOO

You're only a kind person
if you're kind to yourself too
otherwise you've fallen
into the people-pleasing trap
and that will break your spirit
my friend.

Kindness starts at home
and home starts with you
and you deserve that kindness
as much as any other.

Do not throw your kindness
out into this world
without gifting a little of it your way.

There is a little version of you
who waits deep inside
hoping for it
thirsty for that kindness.

And they cannot accept it from others
until they feel worthy enough
and worthy starts at home too
worthy starts with you.

You're only a kind person
if you're kind to yourself too.

Be kind to yourself too.

DUSTY LENS

When youth was in full bloom
you loved
oh how you loved
almost instantly
with every ounce of your being
you loved
and longed for
and adored.

And often it felt as though that love
could be the very death of you
so deeply were you consumed
by its blaze.

But then along comes the love
for your child
and you realise
almost instantly
that until this moment
you have not known
what true love felt like.

And the world around you changes
almost instantly
as everything comes into view
so clearly
in such sharp focus
as though all this time
you were looking

through a dusty lens.

LOVING

People may put you down for loving too much
for loving the moon and her many faces
for loving the rain and the thunder
and every animal whose path you cross.

People may consider you weak
throwing your love around like confetti
without measure or judgement.

But my friend
you must not hear
their heavy hearts
you must always share
that fountain of love
you so beautifully create
because it is a substance of great power.

And if people can hate
for no good reason
and they do
then you can love
for no good reason too
and it is vital that you do.

Vital that you do.

OCEANS AND STREAMS

You've crossed so many oceans
for those who called you near
you've shown up for the bad times
digging deep to bring them cheer

You've carried others' burdens
your back already strained
you've given joy and comfort
your soul is truly drained

And in this life of giving
you have failed to fully see
that when you need their friendship
they won't push their boat to sea

You stay there on your island
your rescue but a dream
stop crossing stormy oceans
for those who won't cross streams.

IT WILL BE YOU

And then one day it will be you
you will choose yourself
you will extend a hand
and a warm invitation
usher yourself in
to a welcoming home
and you will see
a little too late
but strangely
right on time
that it was *always you*
that it was always a home
missing a heart
without you in it
that you were choosing
so many others
over the one
you needed
all along
you.

FOR A LIFETIME

If you plan to love someone for a lifetime
be prepared to grieve
for the versions of themselves
they will outgrow.

If you plan to love someone for a lifetime
be prepared to fall in love anew
with the versions of themselves
they will grow into.

And if you plan to *be loved*
for a lifetime
be ready to love yourself
in versions old and new

for only those who love within
can happily accept love.

And as with everything
everything
in life
change is constant

and nothing stays the same.

TO LOVE YOURSELF

To love yourself is ugly
it requires some breaking down
of walls and masks and filters
that time has built around

It comes when tears and anger
have all been flushed away
with comparison and judgement
and other peoples' say

It's a lengthy work in progress
and it doesn't happen fast
but with every little victory
you have built something to last

So chip away your armour
be sure to delve quite deep
self-love may not come easy
but then it's yours to keep.

LET THEM REST

If you love someone
let them rest
without criticism
without judgement
without talk of tasks undone.

For surely
there is no greater act of love
than allowing someone
to seek peace
to find solace
to reap strength
when they are in need.

And if you want to love yourself more
let yourself rest too
without criticism
without judgement
without fear of missing out
on all the *doing*.

To show your love
there is no greater affection
than the power of unapologetic rest.

ONLY YOU

Only you will ever know the real you.

Everyone else sees a version of you
a version created in their mind
through their filters
using their own
experiences and judgements
to mould you.

You may think they see
what you know
about yourself
but they don't.

Everyone you have ever met
holds a version of you
in their memory.
None of them are real.

It is a special moment
when this truth sinks in
because at last you realise
you've a very unique
thing going on
with yourself.

So many versions of you exist
in very many places
but only you
will know the real one.

Now if that is not a relationship
well worth treasuring
what is?

STRANGERS

Some of the most supportive people
I have ever encountered in this life
have owed me nothing.

Veritable strangers.

Souls who reached
across silent divides
and took my hand
offering me solace
where none existed.

And they delivered
and they meant it
and that instant connection *prevailed*
against the odds.

Do not imagine your tribe
must show their worth
with the passage of time
or the to-ing and fro-ing of favours.

Sometimes that spark is just raw and real
pure and unexplainable
you must go with it
allow the beauty to unfold.

Some of the most supportive people
I have encountered in this life
have owed me nothing.

Veritable strangers
who fast became friends.

TO LOVE YOUR DAUGHTER

If you want to love your daughter
love *yourself*.

And let her grow
nourished by acceptance
from the inside
of her world
a front row seat.

And let her know
that this worth
should not be tied to false idols
or societal expectations.

Let her see
how it matters not
your size
your success
or your popularity
for those things wane
with the tides and the moon
as all things must
but never your worth
that is the rock
the mountain range
that is base camp.

If you want to love your daughter
love yourself
for there is no better gift
lesson or accolade
to pass on
than this.

LITTLE MAN

I remember that cheek
when it curved like a bow
and those arms now so strong
once soft as fresh dough

I remember the smell
of your baby sweet head
and the sound of your breath
as you slumbered in bed

I will never forget
how your hand fit in mine
and your arms wrapped around me
all of the time

You are grown now my love
and it fills me with joy
to see how you've journeyed
to man from sweet boy

But that cheek with its plumpness
still lives in my heart
I'll never forget you were mine
at the start.

DEAR SISTER

We have not always seen
eye to eye
that much is true.

But we have seen
each other's lives
from the inside
and we know
each other's hearts
from that perspective too.

Not eye to eye perhaps
but heart to heart for sure.

And that connects us
across oceans and timelines.

The threads that bind us
dear sister
are strong
buried deep
complicated
and solid.

The lasting kind
not the easy kind
the best things
never are.

I don't think friendships

are given enough credit

they are the unwritten love stories

each and every one

DANDELION SEEDS

Some people think of roses
when they talk about love
but I think of dandelion seeds.

Not rare
but everywhere.

Their ethereal beauty
so utterly delicate
entirely vulnerable
unafraid to be scattered
across land and time
spreading themselves far and wide
creating more love wherever they land
bringing light and beauty
to the most parched ground.

Some people think of roses
when they talk about love
but I think of dandelion seeds.

And I let myself go
to the wind
knowing
there is no end.

Love just grows
not rare
but everywhere.

LOVE WILL NOT SPOIL

Dear Mama
you cannot love your baby spoiled
it is simply not possible.

Too much love does not exist.

Love has never ruined a gracious heart
or caused a wholesome soul to fester.

Love has never made a monster
or raised a careless mate.

Love can only create
more love
in its wake.

And too much of it is not a thing.

If your baby craves your warmth
in the cold and dark of night
snuggle in
these days are not for long
and that love will create safety
which breeds esteem
which breeds self-love
and self-love is where all love grows best.

Dear Mama
you cannot love your baby spoiled
too much love is not a thing.

GO LITTLE

When everything feels too big
go little.

When the overwhelm
is dragging you down
go down.

Make yourself small
make your world small
wrap yourself in a blanket
and take every little task
one tiny crumb at a time.

You can't outrun that tsunami
nor can you swim it.

You must do as it wishes.

Let the wave wash you along
till finally
you open your eyes
on a beach
blinking at the sunlight
as it caresses your skin.

When everything feels too big
go little.

TO A FLOWER

Mother Nature made so much
to be proud and grateful for
the peaks of snowy mountains
the seas on sandy shores

Dotting glitter in the sky
to shine through darkest night
she drew with every colour
creating rainbows with the light

But she spent much of her time
blooming buds to bring true pleasure
every shape, every colour, every size
each one a treasure

A bloom for all occasions
to stir emotions with each scent
a bloom for every message
a heart could need to send

It's her flowers that she gifted
to say words we cannot find
those flowers keep us lifted
when we face the hardest times.

ATTENTION

Whatever you focus
your attention on
grows

so with this in mind
why not start ignoring
all the things
that bring you down
and start focusing instead
on the stuff that charges you up
from the inside out
things you truly *love*.

It's your life
your world
you can decide how to see
any part of it differently.

Same goes for yourself.

As game changers go
this is the one.

LET JOY STAY HIGH

If you have a chance
to let loose today
to unclench the safety bar
throw your hands high
in the air
take it.

The world will always be a boiling pot
of good, bad and ugly.

A confusing kaleidoscope
of all emotions at once.

But you must make sure joy
stays high in the mix.

Joy, hope and love.

These are the ones
which will keep the balance from
ever shifting downwards.

So feel them
and wave them aloft
for others to see too.

Do not hide them away my friends
they must be celebrated
at every opportunity.

THE LOST FRIENDS

It is a universal truth
that we will meet
fall in love with
and drift apart
from many friends
in our lifetime.

And it is okay
to feel bereft
when we reminisce
on the bonds once beautiful
now so broken.

Because someone once said
reason, season, lifetime
and I think they were very wise.

Those you need
really need
those you are supposed
to see the finish line with
are still here
and the rest must be released
with love.

They taught you more
than you may know.

Let them go.

ALONE IS NOT UNLOVED

It is quite simply untrue
that you must marry
to be loved
for a lifetime.

It is quite simply untrue
that you must live as half of a two
to be complete
in this life.

It is quite simply true
that love comes in many forms
yet we seem to place measure
on only one
the love from our partner.

When we should be placing measure
on all the love we have in general
and especially that for ourselves.

Alone is not unloved my friends.

Alone is not unloved.

WHEREVER I GO

I wonder if you know
that I carry you with me
wherever I go

I wonder if you see
that you're very much
a part of me

I wonder if
you feel the same

I wonder
do we share that pain

I wonder if you know
that I carry you with me
wherever I go.

THE CHOOSING

To the parents
who give safety and
warmth
to a child
left in the cold
I thank you
for your contribution
to this world
for your love
for your *choice*
for your giant heart.

It's in the *choosing*
that love somehow
becomes blood
that parent and child
somehow
become linked
in more ways
than we can explain.

Because what more
can one soul do for another
than to *choose* them.

It is the ultimate act of care.

TOMORROW

You've closed your bright eyes now my love
given your all to this day
and now you're sleeping so soundly
there's so much that I want to say

I'm sorry I didn't play longer
you begged me for just one more game
I regret all the times I ignored you
I'm truly awash with the shame

And sometimes I know I get shouty
your bottom lip wobbles with tears
I pray that you know I don't mean it
it's one of my deepest dark fears

Tomorrow, I promise to linger
and stare at the bugs on the ground
I promise to try not to rush you
and listen to your every sound

I want you to know you're amazing
a tonic for every day
you show me what life is about love
you're blazing bright, leading the way

Your laughter can fill me with gladness
your smile more bright than the sun
I could stare at your profile for hours
my beautiful, smart little one

Please never doubt how much I love you
the sight of you makes my heart swell
the way that your cheek curves so plumply
that wonderful, baby soft smell

So sleep tight my angel, I'm with you
dream of a life filled with fun
if I could stop things that may hurt you
I'd do so my brave little one

Storms may rage over our castle
and life can be so full of harm
but all I can do is embrace you
you're safe here in my loving arms

I'd give all I have to protect you
and bring you a world that is safe
till then I can only just hold you
and wish all the badness away.

FROSTING

Love can arrive
wearing many a disguise
but never
does it look
like an expensive gift
or a romantic weekend
for two.

That's just frosting.

You're far more likely
to find real love
in a cup of tea
made just for you
exactly the way you like it.

HOW YOU GROW

The bravest thing you can do
is be kind to yourself
when you feel
you deserve it
the *least*.

When you are imperfect
when you have failed.

When you are off track
out of whack
and flawed.

If you can find
that grain of kindness
for your most unloveable self
it will land
like blessed raindrops
on a parched plant.

And that my friend

is how you grow.

ROT

I'm no expert
but I'm pretty sure
that anything eaten
with *love*
made
with love
is fairly good for you.

And anything
eaten with guilt
and self loathing
will rot you
from the inside out.

I'm no expert
but I'm fairly certain
that love
in its purest form
is the best medicine

known to humankind.

UNSPOKEN TRUTHS

I think it is an unspoken truth
that a very large allowance
of the romance in your life
will come from other women.

And that's okay.

Not only is that okay
it is *vital*
because we *know*
intuitively
what is needed
at the right times
and we are connected
to one another
with silvery threads of friendship
that stitch core to core
gut to gut
and heart to heart.

I think it is an unspoken truth
that a very large allowance
of the romance in your life
will come from other women.

And that's okay.

INTO THE GROUND

I am sorry if someone
took your precious heart
and walked it into the ground.

I am sorry if they smashed it
and stamped it to smithereens
leaving you shattered
a million unrecognisable pieces.

But whilst you lay there
pushed deep into the earth
something miraculous occurred
you did not die
you planted yourself
and you let those pieces root
like seeds into the soil.

And every day
you bravely sought the sun
and warmly welcomed the rain
until very soon you were growing
renewed and stronger still.

I am sorry that someone
took your precious heart
and walked it in the ground
but I am so very proud

of how you climbed back out.

CLOSE TO THE SUN

Perhaps your wings were clipped
from the start
or badly beaten down
by someone's hardened heart?

And yet despite this
your beautiful wings have now grown
tentatively
and you are afraid
to try them out
in case you soar
too close to the sun.

You should know my love
that your wings
will not only take you
to wherever you dream to be
they will also take you *away*
from somewhere
you do not feel safe.

And that going close to the sun
is what you are here to do.

So you needn't be afraid.

LOVE IS ALL AROUND

You must believe in love
and if one day you don't
go to the arrivals gate
and watch people greet
their loved ones.

It is life-giving oxygen
for a heart running fast
out of care.

Husbands and wives
friends reunited
grandparents wrapped
in much missed soft kisses
and smothered entirely in joy.

Parents desperately awaiting
their young
flying back to the nest
after their first flight
out into this dangerous world.

Gratitude, relief
happiness and love.
Everywhere.

You must believe in love
my friend
it truly is all around.

TORCH IN MY POCKET

Like a little torch in my pocket
the image of your smile
can light my way
the words you pour upon me
when I let my troubles out
will stay with me
until my dying day

Like a little blanket in my backpack
your laughter warms
the cockles of my heart
I wrap your love around me
and I snuggle in so close
I feel you still
and yet we're far apart

Like a little torch in my pocket
your friendship stops the dark
from closing in
I understand the power
of a bond so deeply made
you and I against the world
we'll always win.

how amazing is the truth

that this planet has existed

for billions of years

and I get to spend my few with you

SOMEONE

Find someone who hears you
even when you're silent.

Someone who sees
your spark waning
and wants to learn
how to restart its light.

Find someone who understands
that your soul will never age
or lose its beauty
for even Father Time
cannot steal that.

Find someone who likes you
as you *are*
in all your glory
and doesn't want to change you
for their *better*.

Find someone like this
and hold their hand
through the good
the bad and the ugly.

And if you cannot find this other
do it for yourself
until you do.

Because you very much deserve
true love.

LOVE IS THE GOAL

Teach your little girls
to be happy on their own
to feel worthy in a crowd
whether single or attached.

Teach your little girls
that a life unwed
is better by far
than wasting a single day
in an unhappy home.

Teach your children
that no pairing is worth
detaching parts of your soul
to better fit into.

Teach them that love
is not always pretty
but it is always respectful
always *safe*.

And if their instincts
start to feel
any other way
they can leave
they can *always* leave
and they must
leave.

Teach your children
to feel complete
on their own
and remind them
they are already loved
by you
in glorious technicolour.

And that's the goal.

That's the goal.

DIDN'T WASTE A DAY

At some point
you will be confronted
with your end of days
and you will stop looking forward
and start looking back
back over your journey
here on this earth.

You will scour and search
through the databases
of your mind
to count all the ways
in which you *mattered*.

You will see faces
young and old
tiny hands
and curled up toes
morning hugs
and bedtime kisses
troubles halved
by sharing woes.

You will hear laughter
and sweet music
songs sung loud
through happy tears
as the movie
of your life
plays loudly
through your years.

Over and above anything
you will find
in the albums
of your mind
is love.

So much love
felt in so many different ways.

And you will know as you look back

that you didn't waste a day.

SHE SCREAMED

If you've survived
a toxic relationship
chances are
your soul and you
may be very disconnected.

She screamed at you
you see
(*in vain*)
for so very long.

Until she was sure
her screams must be silent
so little notice did you take.

Bridge the gap
right the wrongs
make your apologies.

You pushed her out
but she's still there my friend.

Welcome her in
and make a vow
to listen much harder

next time.

ACKNOWLEGEMENTS

Thank you for buying this book, or if someone has gifted it to you, remember each time you open the pages, how very valued you are. I would love to see you on my social media accounts where we daily remind each other, that no matter what the issue, love is always the answer.

'*What could be a greater act of self-love
than to set yourself free.*

Free to find even more love.

Real love.'

If you have been affected by any of the topics raised in *Love,*
you may find it helpful to talk to your partner, a relative, friend
or reach out to one of the services below. You do not have to be
in a crisis to call, you might just need a listening ear or to find
help for a friend in need.

Mental Health UK
For those looking for help with symptoms
and treatment for mental health conditions as well
as a wide range of support services.
www.mentalhealth-uk.org

Samaritans
Round the clock support for anyone who needs to talk.
www.samaritans.org

Mind
Dedicated to better mental health, Mind provides details of
resources and support in your area.
www.mind.org.uk

COPE Scotland
Tips, resources and a huge range of materials shared on the
website which are geared towards self-care and self-
management of personal wellbeing.
www.cope-scotland.org

Relate
For help with all kinds of relationships, whether they are past,
present or future, problematic or perfect.
www.relate.org.uk

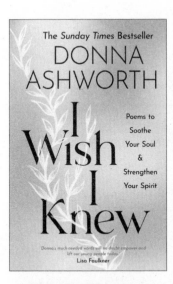

The *Sunday Times* Bestseller
DONNA
ASHWORTH

I Wish I Knew

Poems to Soothe Your Soul & Strengthen Your Spirit

Donna's much-needed words will no doubt empower and lift our young people today.
Lisa Faulkner

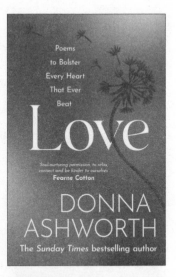

Poems to Bolster Every Heart That Ever Beat

Love

Soul-nurturing permission to relax, connect and be kinder to ourselves.
Fearne Cotton

DONNA
ASHWORTH

The *Sunday Times* bestselling author

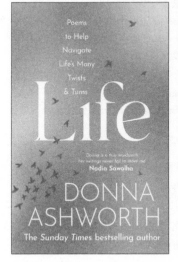

Poems to Help Navigate Life's Many Twists & Turns

Life

Donna is a true wordsmith, her writings never fail to move me.
Nadia Sawalha

DONNA
ASHWORTH

The *Sunday Times* bestselling author

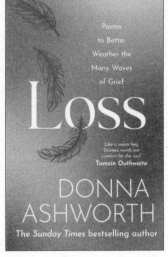

Poems to Better Weather the Many Waves of Grief

Loss

Like a warm hug, Donna's words are comfort for the soul.
Tamzin Outhwaite

DONNA
ASHWORTH

The *Sunday Times* bestselling author

Donna Ashworth is a *Sunday Times* bestselling author and a lover of words who lives happily in the hills of Scotland with her husband, two sons, and Brian and Dave (the dogs). Donna started her social media accounts in 2018 and is astounded daily by the international reach her words have garnered.

"My dream was to connect with women all over the world, so we could look at each other and say *I see you, this is hard* and just generally agree that imperfection is to be celebrated not feared."

When she is not writing, Donna loves to eat, be merry and laugh; believing these to be the best medicines life can offer.

Instagram @DonnaAshworthWords
TikTok @DonnaAshworthWordy
facebook.com/ladiespassiton
www.donnaashworth.com